CANDLEMAKING

Mary Carey

PAN BOOKS LTD · LONDON

ART DIRECTOR: Remo Cosentino
ART ASSISTANT: Barbara Braunstein
PHOTOGRAPHS: George Ancona
EDITOR: Caroline Greenberg

Contents

First British edition published 1973 by Pan Books Ltd, 33 Tothill Street, London SW1

ISBN 0 330 23784 5

© Western Publishing Company, Inc, 1972

PRINTED IN ENGLAND BY CRIPPLEGATE PRINTING CO LTD LONDON & EDENBRIDGE

No one actually needs candles today, so the traditional light has become a decoration, brilliant or subtle, conventional or eccentric, but never dull

Equipment

Strictly speaking, a candle is a piece of wax with a wick embedded in it. Therefore, strictly speaking, one could take a block of paraffin, insert a wick, and call the resulting object a candle. Touch a match to the wick and the thing would burn as candles are supposed to burn. However, even the most undemanding critic wouldn't give a rave review to such a candle, and inserting a wick into paraffin would satisfy no one's creative urge.

If you plan to make candles at all, you owe it to yourself to use the same fine materials that professionals enjoy. Good candlemaking supplies are not very costly, and the results can more than justify the expenditure of a few pounds at your nearby hobby shop.

Wax, Wicking, and Mould

To begin with, provide yourself with a good grade of paraffin and a few metres of wicking. The easiest candle for the novice to make is the poured candle, and for this you will need a mould. Almost anything that can hold melted wax until it hardens can serve as a mould (see pages 30–35), but for the best results you should have at least one finely crafted metal candle mould. These come complete with wick holders, with gaskets or screws for sealing wick holes, and with directions for wicking. If it is cared for properly, a good metal mould will last for ever. A 1 litre (1 quart) square or round metal mould is most satisfactory for first experiments in candlemaking. (As you gain experience and begin to experiment, you will want to try other kinds of moulds and other wicking procedures.)

Stearin

In addition to wax, wick, and mould, you must have stearin. It's a staple with every candlemaker. This substance, derived from fats such as tallow and butterfat, is sold in the form of powdery, white crystals. It is added to melted paraffin to make a finished candle more opaque. Stearin also raises the melting point of paraffin, so that candles do not sag or bend in a warm room. It makes white candles white and coloured candles bright.

Dyes

Special candle dyes should always be used for coloured candles. These are available in several forms: cakes of intensely coloured wax from which small chips can be shaved, granules of wax, liquids, and tablets. Don't try to use food colouring,

Wax, wicking, stearin, mould, mould release, and dyes are basic candle supplies.
You also need a melting pot and a sugar thermometer. The equipment for cutting
wicks, trimming candles, and stirring dyes is probably in your kitchen already.
And don't forget newspapers; no one loves a messy candlemaker

which won't mix with wax, and don't waste time experimenting with crayons. Some crayons contain substances which will cause candles to sputter, and the wax from crayons may not disperse evenly through candle wax.

Mould Release

Nearly every candlemaker uses a mould release of one type or another. The release is applied to the inside of the mould before the candle is poured, just as butter or margarine is rubbed around the inside of a cake pan before the cake batter is poured. After the candle has hardened in the mould, it will slide out more easily if mould release has been used.

Salad oil makes a fairly satisfactory mould release if it is applied sparingly. Any of the ready-made dressings used in cooking will also serve. Hobby shops offer fine silicone sprays especially for candlemaking. When using mould release, it is important not to be too enthusiastic. If you apply too much, droplets may form inside the mould and the finished candle will have little bubbles in the surface. If you use salad oil, wipe the inside of the mould with a tissue before pouring the candle to be sure that you have removed any excess which might mar the candle.

Perfumes

Perfumes are not absolutely necessary in a candle, but they are a nice enhancement. Candle perfumes come in a wide variety, ranging from the familiar bayberry and rose to exotic fragrances like patchouli and frangipani. They are usually oil-based, so that they will blend with wax, and some come complete with directions as to amounts to be added to melted wax. Follow the directions. If you don't have directions, use discretion. A few drops to each kilogram of wax should be enough. You want a subtle aroma, not a candle that will fairly fumigate a house.

Your supplies for candlemaking, then, will include wax, wicking, mould, mould release, stearin, dyes, and perfumes.

Some additional items are required, but these are probably already in your kitchen. Take a quick inventory.

Other Equipment

Do you have a double boiler? You should, since it is safest to melt wax over boiling water. If you don't have a double boiler, you can construct one. Put a trivet in the bottom of a large pan. Pour water into the pan, and then put the pot in which you will melt your wax on the trivet.

You *must* have a sugar thermometer. It is necessary to know the temperature of the melted wax at all times, and there is only one way to do this. Clip a sugar thermometer to the edge of the melting pot or double boiler and watch the thermometer. If you haven't a sugar thermometer, get one. It won't be expensive, and you can't do without it.

You probably already have a water-bath container. This is any vessel, such as a plastic or metal wastepaper basket or a large bucket, which can be partly filled with water. After you have poured hot wax into a mould, you hasten the hardening of the wax by putting the mould into the water bath.

Some moulds tend to float when put into a water bath, so keep a heavy object on hand in case you have to weigh the mould down. Nice clean bricks or large trivets make fine weights for moulds. Electric irons or large books do not make good weights, since electric irons and books should not be accidentally dropped into water baths.

You can, if you wish, pour wax directly from a double boiler or melting pot into a mould, but it is neater, safer, and more satisfactory to use a container with a handle and a pouring lip. A 1 litre (1 quart) pyrex measuring jug makes a perfect pouring container. A kettle with a pouring spout is also fine, although perhaps not as easy to keep clean.

A skewer or ice-pick is a great comfort to any candlemaker, as it can be used to chip wax into small chunks for faster melting. As a candle hardens, a skewer can be inserted into the centre to see if the wax has contracted and pulled away from the wick, leaving a cavity that must be filled. A skewer can also be heated and used as a wick rod to make wick holes in candles which have been moulded without wicks. (If you do not have a skewer or ice-pick, try using a screwdriver – but not too large a screwdriver.)

You will also want a goodly supply of newspapers to spread over your working area, paper towels to wipe things and clean things up, a paring knife, a pair of kitchen shears for cutting wicking, a hammer for breaking up wax, a tablespoon for measuring stearin, and, since you will be working with hot wax, a pair of pot holders or an oven mitt to protect your hands.

And a stove. Of course you have a stove.

Safety

Wax will burn. It would be of no use in candles if it didn't vaporize and burn. This doesn't mean that candlemakers need constantly dread a wax fire, but it does mean that a little care and the observance of a few rules are required.

Basic Safety Rules

First, melt wax over boiling water. Water cannot get hotter than 100° C. Wax will not vaporize and ignite at this temperature, so the candlemaker who uses a double boiler should not have any difficulties.

Always use a sugar thermometer. It isn't necessary to bring wax even to 100° for candlemaking. Watch the thermometer and remove the wax from the heat when it reaches 93°C.

Never, never leave melting wax unattended. Even if you are going to step out of the room for only a second, remove the wax from the stove or turn off the burner under the wax.

See to it that the work area where you pour your candles is several steps removed from the stove. You will cover the work area with newspaper to keep wax off counters and tabletops. If the papers are too close to the stove, they may catch fire.

Wax does not bubble and boil, but it does get hot. Use pot holders or oven mitts when handling melting pots or pouring containers, and use only pouring containers with handles and pouring lips or spouts.

When glazing (see page 25), be sure to allow for displacement. For instance, one way to glaze a candle is to dip it into hot water. Be certain the container in which you have heated the water is big enough, and that it is not too full of water. Otherwise, hot water and wax will spill out over the top as the candle is dipped.

Never dip a candle into *boiling* water. Steam rising from boiling water can be hotter than 100° C, and it can also be invisible – super-heated water vapour. Avoid steam burns. Heat water to boiling, then turn off the stove and allow the water to cool for a few moments before dipping your candle.

The candlemaker who uses hot wax for glazing must be even more careful than the one who uses water. Allow plenty of room for the tide of wax to rise in the container when the candle is dipped, and never glaze a candle in a container which has a flame going under it.

It goes without saying that small children and hot wax do not mix. Until a child is old enough, tall enough, and experi-

For safety's sake, be sure the working area where you will pour wax is at least a metre away from the stove

enced enough to handle ordinary cooking chores, he should not be permitted anywhere near a candlemaking operation.

Special Precautions

If you break – or even bend – any of the above rules, be especially wary.

Many candlemakers decide to do a rush job by melting wax directly over the burner. This is not a good idea, since the wax won't heat as evenly. However, if you do decide to melt wax in this manner, don't leave the wax for a moment. Watch the sugar thermometer like a hawk. You will find the temperature of wax goes up at an astonishing rate. The instant the thermometer hits 93°C, turn off the heat. The wax will then begin to cool, and soon you will have to heat it again. But don't complain. You have to pay for your haste.

Sooner or later, many candlemakers succumb to the temptation to leave wax in the bottom of a melting pot overnight or longer. There is nothing downright sinful about this, but sooner or later the hardened wax will have to be melted again. Naturally, it will melt from the bottom. The liquid wax will then expand and press against the still-solid layer of wax at the top of the melting pot. This pressure should be relieved. Use your skewer to break through the solid wax, and use it early in the melting process. If you wait too long, liquid wax may spurt up through the solid layer and hit you, the kitchen wall, or the stove.

If wax in the melting pot catches fire, smother the flame with a pot lid. Also, keep an open box of baking soda handy

In Case of Accident

Prevention is always the best medicine, but even careful candlemakers can have mishaps. There's no real need for trouble, but it's wise to be prepared.

If the wax in your melting pot catches fire, turn off the heat and put a lid on the pot to smother the flames.

Keep an open box of baking soda ready. If wax spills onto the stove it will almost certainly burn. Turn off the stove and throw handfuls of baking soda onto the burning wax.

The best protection against a wax fire is a chemical fire extinguisher. These aren't expensive, and most people who indulge in candlemaking keep one in their work areas.

Never use water to try to put out a wax fire. Water will only splatter the wax, as it would cooking oil, and spread the fire.

If you do have a fire and it seems that things are getting out of control, don't hesitate. Call the fire service.

And if you should spill hot wax on your hands – or any other part of your anatomy – don't try to wipe it off. Run cold water over the wax. It will harden instantly and can be lifted off. Treat the burned area as you would any scald or burn.

If you get hot wax on your hands, don't try to rub it off. Run cold water on the wax; it will harden and lift off

Waxes and Wicks

Undeniably, the finest candle material is still beeswax. It has a high melting temperature, it is fairly pliable even when it's cold, and it produces its own gentle fragrance when it burns. It is, however, so expensive that it is out of the question for the home candlemaker unless he also happens to keep bees. Today, almost the only place one can see pure beeswax candles is in churches.

This does not mean that beeswax need be completely ignored by the amateur candlemaker. Pre-dyed sheets of beeswax are sold in craft shops and hobby stores, and these can be used to decorate candles. Beeswax is also available in undyed blocks, and some more experienced craftsmen blend beeswax with paraffin to get a scented, long-burning candle. Because beeswax is slightly tacky, it tends to stick to the sides of a mould. If you experiment with beeswax, use mould release and then fill your mould with regular paraffin. Let this set for about ten minutes, then pour out the paraffin that's still liquid. You will have a thin coating of paraffin in the mould; this will prevent the beeswax from sticking and binding the candle to the mould.

Another traditional wax which is still available is bayberry. Like beeswax, it is expensive, since it takes about 4½ kgs (10 lb) of bayberries to produce ½ kg (1 lb) of bayberry wax, but few things are nicer for a special gift on a very special occasion than a bayberry candle.

There are special floral or sculpture waxes available in craft shops. These are usually blends of paraffin and beeswax and are intended for use by the craftsman who wants to fashion wax flowers or sculpture decorations for candles. These waxes must be warmed before they are used, but they become pliable and easy to work before they become liquid.

Paraffin Waxes

For all but the most special, precious candles, paraffin wax is completely satisfactory. There are low-temperature paraffin waxes which melt at about 54°C., and there are waxes that remain solid until heated to 74°C or over, but the most useful and easily obtainable wax is the medium-temperature wax which becomes liquid at about 63°C. Some shops carry a medium-temperature wax to which stearin has already been added; this is suitable for most candlemaking. However, for some candles and for glazes, stearin isn't desirable.

The most versatile wax, therefore, is the fine-quality medium-temperature paraffin which is sold in 5 kg (11 lb) slabs. When it comes from the store it is grey-white and semi-translucent and has a faintly slippery, soapy feeling. The candlemaker can add stearin himself to change the grey-white colour to white, and to make this wax more opaque and harder. (The addition of candle dye, of course, will change the colour completely.)

Measuring Wax and Stearin

There are no very precise formulas for deciding the proportion of stearin to wax in candles. In a way, candlemaking defies formulas, and most candlemakers have their own ideas about how things should be done. The beginner will want to have some grip on the situation, however, and should assume that for a white candle, at least 54 mls (3 tbs) of stearin should be added to each ½ kg (1 lb) of wax. Dyed candles require only one or two tablespoons for ½ kg (1 lb). If you miscalculate, you will see why when your candle is unmoulded. You have not put in enough stearin if your candle is soapy and too soft. You have put in too much stearin if your candle is brittle and tends to have splintery cracks. You can vary the amount of stearin when the next candle is made.

Add no stearin at all to wax which is used for a glaze.

Cutting chunks of wax from a thick, 5 kg (11 lb) slab can be a problem, and the solution depends on the temperament and strength of the candlemaker. Some people simply hold the wax in one hand, grasp a hammer in the other, and beat the slab to bits. Some people put the wax slab into a sack or an old pillow case and beat that with a hammer. Some people measure their waxen slabs into precise quarters and delicately chip these away with a skewer.

Measuring wax and deciding on the amount of stearin to be added can be difficult. If you have kitchen scales, your problem is solved. If you don't, there are some rules of thumb which can be helpful:

- One 5 kg (11 lb) slab of wax equals 4·5 litres (4 quarts) of liquid wax, more or less.
- If you are using a 1 litre (1 quart) mould, hack off about one-fourth of the wax from your 5 kg (11 lb) mould. This will give you about 1·5 kg (3 lb) of wax.
- Remember that you will never come out even to the last decimal point. Don't let this worry you. A few grammes one way or another will not make any difference.
- Also remember that after you have moulded your candle, you will have wax left over. This is not a problem. Save the wax for your next candlemaking session; it won't spoil.

Most paraffin wax comes in 5 kg (11 lb) slabs. Other sizes are available, such as the 5½ kg (12 lb) scored slab shown above. The size of the wicking you select depends on the size of your mould

Wicks

Choosing the proper wick can be even trickier than measuring wax. Here, experimentation really comes in, and you will not know how successful you have been until you light your finished candle.

For most candles which are poured into regular candle moulds, a plain braided wick is used. The size of the wick depends on the size of the mould. For candles 50 mm (2 ins) in diameter or smaller, use a small wick. A medium square-braid wick is suitable for candles from 50–100 mm (2–4 ins) in diameter, and any wax pillar candle bigger than 100 mm (4 ins) requires a larger wick. Trial and error is the best way to decide which wick to use with which mould. The mould manufacturers attempt to make it as easy as possible for their customers. Each commercial mould comes complete with a length of wicking which should be the right size for the mould. Try to match this size wick for future castings in the mould.

Wire-core Wicks

Some candles are moulded without wicks, and the wick is added after the candle has hardened (stack candles, for example, on page 40). For this type of candlemaking, a metal-core wick is indispensable. Like the regular braided wick, the metal-core wick is made of cotton yarn, and it comes in several sizes. In the centre of each of these wicks is a fine wire – magnesium, lead, or steel. This wire, which makes the wick fairly rigid, is so slender that it will vaporize and burn when the candle is lighted. To use the wire-core wick, the candlemaker heats a skewer and applies it to the finished candle to make a wick hole. He then inserts the metal-core wick into the hole (see photograph) and seals the hole with a small amount of warm wax.

Wire-core wicks are slightly rigid, and can be added to a candle after it is unmoulded. Make a hole in the candle with a hot skewer or ice-pick, dip the wick into warm wax, pull it taut, and then insert it into the wick hole

Colour

Candle dyes are pure pigment suspended either in wax or in oil. They are so concentrated that a red dye can appear almost black and a bright yellow may look like a very deep brown.

Unless you plan to go into candlemaking on a truly enormous scale, do not attempt to bypass the craft shops and mix your own dyes. The pigment is a fine powder, and the slightest draught will set it swirling through the air. Even professionals have had their troubles with pigments, and only a mother can love a bright blue candlemaker.

Use the dyes which are sold especially for candles. The range of colours available is enormous. You can purchase deep red, hot pink, orange, yellow, lavender, purple, bright blue, brown, black, and almost any shade in between.

Mixing Colours

If you wish, you can start out with the three primary colours: red, yellow, and blue. Remember the art classes you had in primary school and blend your own shades. For example:

Pink is red plus white, so for a pink candle add only a tiny amount of red dye to your candle wax and increase the amount of stearin you use.

The novice candlemaker can start with as few as three colours. Just remember the colour wheel (above): combine yellow and blue to get green; blue and red for purple; and red mixed with yellow for orange. You can vary the intensity of colour in dyed wax by using greater or lesser amounts of dye (left)

There is a certain amount of guesswork in all candlemaking. What colour will the finished candle be when it is unmoulded? You can get some idea by dropping a bit of wax into a cup of cold water. As the wax hardens, you can tell approximately how intense the colour will be in the finished candle

Orange is red plus yellow.

Blue and yellow will give you green – light green or dark green, depending on the proportion of yellow to blue.

Red and blue equals purple.

Green and red produce brown.

If you find the dyes too brilliant and you wish to mute the colour of your finished candle, add a bit of black.

Adventure with colour all you please. Mix and blend to your heart's content. But don't be hasty when putting dye into melted wax. The dye is extremely strong, and a tiny bit at a time should be added. It is easy to put dye into wax, but it's impossible to get it out again once it's there, so proceed with care.

Testing for Colour

The colour of the melted wax in the double boiler or melting pot will not be the true colour of the finished candle. As the wax sets in the mould and becomes solid and opaque, the dye colour will become deeper and richer. Some experts recommend testing colour by dropping a spoonful of dyed wax onto a white surface – a saucer, perhaps, or the top of the refrigerator. When the wax hardens, the colour will be a shade or two lighter than it will appear in the finished candle, since not that much wax is involved. However, this method will give you an approximate idea of the colour your candle will be.

An alternate testing method – and one which will relieve you of the chore of scraping wax off the saucer or the refrigerator – is to drop a spoonful of wax into a cup of cold water. The wax will harden immediately, and you can see the true colour you will obtain. But again, this small bit of hardened wax will probably be lighter than the entire finished candle.

Casting a Candle: Basic Steps

Before you begin, assemble your supplies and prepare your work area. The work area is the area where you will pour wax into the mould, put the mould in the water bath, and, later, unmould the candle. For safety's sake, this area should be at least a metre removed from the stove.

Cover the area – counter or tabletop – with newspapers. Also, spread newspapers on the floor in front of the work area to catch any stray wax which may spill in the candlemaking process. (No matter how careful you are, there's probably going to be *some* spilled wax.)

Check your supplies against the following list. You should have:

Wax
Wicking
Mould
Stearin
Dyes
Mould release
Perfumes
Double boiler or melting pot and pan
Sugar thermometer
Water-bath container

Weight for holding the mould down in the water bath
Pouring container, such as a pyrex jug. It must have a handle and a pouring lip
Wick rod (skewer, ice-pick or screwdriver)
Paper towels and newspapers
Pot holders or oven mitts

In addition, you will want a **hammer**, to help break chunks of wax from your 5 kg (11 lb) slab, a **paring knife,** if you are using a dye which comes in the form of a solid cube of wax, **scissors** for cutting wicking, and an old **tablespoon** for measuring stearin, mixing in dyes, and ladling out dyed wax for the colour test.

Don't forget to open a box of baking soda.

Melting the Wax

The first step in candlemaking is to break a suitable amount of wax from the 5 kg (11 lb) slab. Break the wax into small chunks for quicker melting.

Put water in the bottom of your double boiler, put wax chunks in the top and place over the heat. As the wax begins to melt, slip the sugar thermometer onto the edge of the double boiler or the melting pot so you can keep track of the temperature of the wax at all times.

Wax should always be melted over boiling water, and the ideal melting pot is a double boiler. Break wax into small chunks for quicker melting

While wax is melting, prepare mould. First, spray it with a mould release or coat it with salad oil

Next, insert wick into mould. This commercial metal mould is sealed at the bottom with a rubber gasket

Fasten the wick to the wick holder. Be sure wick is in the centre of the mould or your candle will burn unevenly

While you are wicking your mould, keep an eye on the sugar thermometer in your melting wax

When wax is at 82–87°C, add stearin — three tablespoons to a pound of wax for a white candle, less for a dyed one

Add dye, a tiny bit at a time. Test for finished colour by dropping a spoonful of wax into a cup of water

Turn off the burner or remove the melting pot from the stove, then add perfume just before pouring candle

Before putting melted wax into a pouring container, wipe melting pot to keep drops of water out of the wax

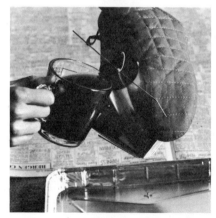

Use an oven mitt when pouring warm wax into a mould; tilt the mould to keep air bubbles from forming in your candle

Once you have started melting wax, do not leave the kitchen. Check the sugar thermometer often, and also make sure that the water under the melting pot or in the bottom of the double boiler has not boiled away.

Preparing the Mould – and Wicking

While the wax is melting, prepare the mould.

First, spray the inside of the mould with a commercial release or coat it with salad oil. Make sure that you don't over-use the release. A very thin coat is adequate.

Next, insert a wick into the mould. All commercial moulds come with instructions for wicking, and these should be read carefully. The wicking process, however, is usually the same for all moulds:

Cut a piece of wicking which is several centimetres longer than the mould.

If you have a mould which has come with a retainer disc (a rubber gasket), thread the wick through the hole in the bottom of the mould and make a knot in the wick below the hole. Slide the retainer disc onto the wick between the knot and the hole and pull the wick up through the mould until the retainer disc and the knot are held firmly against the bottom of the mould. Place the wick holder across the top of the mould and secure the wick to this.

The wick should be positioned so that it is in the centre of the mould. It should not sag or bend, but it should not be pulled too tight or the retainer disc may spread, letting melted wax escape through the bottom of the mould.

If your mould has a retainer screw for sealing the bottom, you will find it easier to thread the wick through the wick hole; pull it up through the mould and fasten it to the wick holder. Then draw the wick until it is tight, but not too tight, insert the retainer screw into the wick hole, wind the wick around the retainer screw, and tighten the screw with a screwdriver.

Mould sealer – a puttylike substance – is often recommended for sealing the bottoms of moulds which have retainer screws. Masking tape can also be used.

For a fine, even finish on a candle, it is wise to pour melted wax into a warm mould. Heat metal moulds by putting them into a warm oven for a few minutes. The key word is 'warm'. The oven should not be hot. Turn it to the lowest temperature, put the mould on the grid well away from the floor of the oven, and leave the oven door open. Fine metal moulds are put together with solder, and you don't want to melt the solder and ruin the mould. Also, you don't want to heat the mould to the point where it will be difficult to handle.

Use mould sealer (a putty-like substance) or masking tape to seal the bottoms of moulds that have retainer screws

A fine glaze can be obtained by dipping a candle into hot wax. The eggshell candles shown below were moulded of white wax. Adding a glaze of coloured wax gives a beautiful, translucent Easter-egg effect.

When glazing a candle, remember to use plenty of extra wick (the best and safest way to dip a candle is by the wick). Also, allow for displacement: the level of hot wax in the glazing container will rise as the candle is lowered into it. As the amateur candlemaker becomes more proficient and strives for special finishes on his candles, he may decide to fashion a special glazing container. These are usually several centimetres in diameter, but quite deep – 46 cms (1½ ft) or more – so the candle-maker can dip his candle without fear of hot wax running out over the top

Now put cool – not cold – water in the water-bath container.

While you have been preparing the mould, you have also been watching the sugar thermometer. When the wax reaches a temperature of about 82–88°C, add stearin – 54 mls (3 tbs) to a ½ kg (1 lb) of wax for a white candle, and 36 mls (2 tbs) for a coloured one.

Stir in the stearin and add dye, a tiny bit at a time.

When the dye is completely dispersed through the melted wax, test for colour either by dropping the wax onto a white surface or by putting some wax into a cup of water.

When your wax reaches 93°C, remove it from the heat immediately.

Pouring

You are now ready to pour the candle. (If you are going to add perfume, now is the time; follow the directions on the bottle.)

Pouring will be done in the work area, away from the stove.

It is important that not a single drop of water gets into the wax, so remove any condensed moisture from the bottom of the melting pot or double boiler with paper towels.

If the melting pot has a pouring lip or spout, pour directly from the pot into the warm metal mould. If the melting pot does not have a pouring lip, use a pouring container which does – and the 1 litre (1 quart) pyrex measuring jug, with its wide top, is perfect for this purpose. (To prevent the wax from cooling too quickly in the cup, you can warm the jug in the oven at the same time as you warm the mould. Then pour the melted wax from the melting pot into the pyrex jug.)

Reserve a small amount of wax in the melting pot – a half to one cup will be sufficient – and put the melting pot back onto the heated water.

Use oven mitts or pot holders to hold the warm mould and the pouring container.

Tilt the mould slightly and pour melted wax down the side of the mould to prevent air bubbles from forming. Fill the mould to within a couple of centimetres of the top, or until you have a candle as tall or short as you desire – considering the size of the mould, of course.

Pouring Temperature

Wax poured into a metal mould should be about 82° to 88°C. It should never be hotter than 93°C. If you pour the wax when it is too hot, you may pit the surface of the candle with steam bubbles. If you let the wax get too cold before pouring, you may have air bubbles in the candle.

The Water Bath

After pouring the wax into the mould, set the mould in the water bath to harden. The water in the water-bath container should be deep enough to reach almost to the top of the mould, but not so deep that water will run over into the mould. If you have miscalculated and the water in the container is not quite deep enough, don't attempt to add more after the mould is in the container. You don't want to get water into the mould, and you don't want little wavy lines in the finished candle – and either of these things may happen if you try to add water after the mould is in the bath.

Weigh the mould down if necessary.

Filling 'Well Areas'

After the candle has cooled in the water bath for about half an hour, reheat the wax you have reserved in the melting pot.

You will see that a scum has formed on top of the candle. Insert an icepick or skewer into the candle next to the wick two or three times to break this scum and relieve the surface tension of the wax. A cavity in the candle, called a well area, will be apparent. This is caused by the contraction of the wax as it cools. Fill this cavity with the wax you have reserved. Use the pyrex jug or the pouring container with lip or spout to fill the well area. Don't add so much wax that it rises beyond the first pouring, or the wax may seep down between the mould and the candle, ruining the surface of the candle.

Wait another half hour and again use the skewer to test for cavities. If any appear, refill the well areas.

In another half-hour, test again for cavities and refill any well areas.

After two to three hours, remove the mould from the water bath. Let the candle continue to cool inside the mould for another six to eight hours. It should be completely cold to the touch before you attempt to unmould the candle. Most candlemakers let pillar candles cool overnight and then unmould them.

Unmoulding

Unmoulding should be simple if you have used a mould release. Undo the gasket and knot at the bottom of the mould, or remove the masking tape and unscrew the retaining screw. Remove the wick holder. Turn the mould upside down and tap it gently on a surface which is covered with some padding (such as a folded towel or a piece of old sheeting folded several times). The candle should slide out easily.

If the candle does not release from the mould immediately, don't try to force it by hammering on the mould. You will only

The water in the water bath should be cool but not cold, and deep enough to reach to the level of the wax

After candle has cooled in the bath, break the surface tension with an ice-pick or skewer and fill cavities with warm wax

moulds   Variations

plastic { star   - curling, or et chopping down sides after dipping
         { square
         (round
          polygon -
metal   - sphere.
glass   long
          button candles
          sand candles
          christmas puddings. (need to buy modelling wax for
                               leaves and berries.)

damage the mould. Instead, put the mould into the refrigerator for fifteen or twenty minutes and chill it slightly. (Don't use the freezer. Candles which have been chilled too severely in refrigerators or in ice-cold water baths may develop unsightly cracks called thermal fractures.)

When the candle is chilled, again tap the mould on the padded surface. The candle should be released.

If no amount of persuasion succeeds in getting the candle out of the mould, you can release it by pouring hot water over the mould. The wax adhering to the walls of the mould will melt slightly and the candle will slide out. The candle will not have a fine, smooth surface, but you will have saved the mould for future use and you can always melt the damaged candle down and try again.

Since most moulds have seams, your candle will probably have one or more seam lines on it. Remove these by sliding a paring knife along the lines. A feather touch is required for this operation, since you don't want to gouge the candle.

Glazing

Candles poured in good metal moulds usually don't require glazing, but if you wish to glaze a candle, do it at this point, before trimming off the extra wick. Holding the candle by the wick, dip it quickly into either hot water or hot wax. (See page 22.)

A reminder: Wax used for glazing should not contain stearin, since a glaze should be translucent. Also, make sure there is room in the container for the water or wax to rise as the candle is dipped.

Finishing

After glazing, let the surface of the candle get completely cold and hard.

Finish the candle by trimming the extra wick from top and bottom. It is unlikely that the bottom of the candle will be absolutely even. Correct this by using a cheese grater to trim off excess wax, then smoothing the bottom of the candle by rubbing it gently on a heated skillet.

If the surface of the candle has been marred by handling, rub away the imperfections with an old nylon stocking.

Use mould release so that your candle will slide out of the mould easily. Don't try to force it by banging the mould

If the finished candle has a seam line from the mould, you can gently smooth it away with a paring knife

A Candle Is for Burning

Candles are more beautiful when they are burning. People look better by candlelight, too. Don't try to save the candles you have made. Unless you want to give them as gifts, use them and enjoy them. Touch a match to the wick and see what happens.

If you have judged correctly as to the relative size of mould and wick, there will be a lovely glow and a minimum of dripping. If you have made a miscalculation, it will show up when the candle is burned.

If your candle flame burns down immediately into the candle, is drowned in melted wax and goes out, your wick is too small. You can make a note of this, and use a slightly larger wick the next time you cast a candle in that particular mould.

If the flame flares up and melts out the sides of the candle, the wick is too large. Use a smaller one next time.

If the wick burns part way down the candle, then suddenly blazes, drops over, and burns through the wall of the candle, causing hot wax to cascade out, you probably have an air pocket inside the candle. Next time, be more careful when filling well areas.

Do not be distressed if any of these things happen when you light your finished candle. You will learn from your small mistakes, and small mistakes in wax are not large disasters. If you can't tolerate a drooping or drowning candle, break it up, retrieve the wick, melt down the wax, and begin again.

One candle which will sooner or later drown its own flame is the large-diameter wax pillar. A candle which is seven, ten or twelve centimetres in diameter will not consume itself entirely even when a large wick is used. Instead, the wick burns down, causing a cavity in the centre of the candle, and the outer walls of the candle remain solid.

If a large-diameter candle is especially lovely and you want to keep it forever, you can. After the wick has burned down an inch or two below the top of the candle, blow out the flame. Scoop out extra wax before it has a chance to harden. Into the resulting cavity, insert a votive light in a glass container. Light the votive light, burn it until it is used up, then replace it with another votive light. You can keep your large candle as long as you like and burn it as often as you please.

Since there are few set rules about candles, there is no set rule that large-diameter candles must be preserved like family heirlooms. You can disregard the votive lights and use the big candle as a glow candle. When the wick has burned down a few centimetres – and threatens to expire in a small sea of wax – blow out the flame. Use a steel spoon to remove the soft, warm wax from around the wick. Do this with care, so as not to break off the wick. Then relight the candle. The flame will glow softly through the wax walls of the candle.

If you follow this routine, you will eventually have a deep well in the large-diameter candle. Use a long match – one of those made especially for lighting fires in fireplaces – to light the candle without burning your fingers.

Whatever you do, never drop match stubs onto the top of a candle. The stubs will soak up wax and become extra wicks – giving much more flame and much more mess than you need or want.

Helpful Hints

Candlemaking is a creative occupation, and like many creative occupations, it can be messy. The candlemaker is apt to have wax on his shoes, just as the painter is apt to have daubs of colour on his shirts. The candlemaker will wear old shoes, therefore, as well as old clothes. But unlike the painter or the sculptor, the candlemaker does not often work in a special studio. He works in a kitchen, and it behoves him to tidy up after he finishes work.

The first rule to remember when cleaning up after making candles is: *Never pour wax down a drain.* Woe to the craftsman who ignores this warning. The wax will harden immediately in the pipes and the plumber will have to be summoned.

Leftover Wax

There will be wax left over; there is *always* wax left over. Heat this in the melting pot, then pour it into a square sandwich tin which has been coated with mould release. When it has hardened in the tin, turn it out, break it into chunks, and put it away to use another day. To prevent it from getting dusty, wrap it in plastic, or store it in a jar with a good lid.

If part of your original slab of wax remains intact, wrap that in plastic, too, before putting it away.

If you have used hot water to glaze a candle, let the water get cold. Some wax will have melted and mixed with the water. When the water is cold, this wax will rise to the top and solidify. It can be lifted off, broken up, and stored away.

Cleaning Your Equipment

Clean the melting pot or double boiler, your skewer, and all other utensils by heating them in a warm oven. Set the oven at low, cover a shelf with aluminium foil to catch any wax drippings, and let the wax melt off the utensils onto the foil.

When the utensils are warm and apparently wax free, wipe them with a paper towel. Then wash them with hot water.

Purists and demon housekeepers clean their moulds after finishing their candles. The process is the same as for utensils and melting pots. Turn the moulds upside down and put them into a warm – not hot – oven on a sheet of aluminium foil. Leave the oven door open so the moulds don't get too hot and the solder doesn't melt.

After the wax has dripped off the moulds, wipe them out with a soft cloth, spray them with mould release to prevent rust, wrap them in plastic, and put them away.

Pour leftover wax into a square sandwich tin. When it is hard, turn it out, break it into chunks, and either wrap it in plastic or put it into a jar to keep it clean

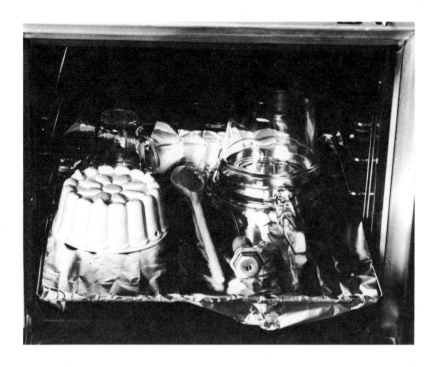

Clean moulds and utensils by putting them on a sheet of aluminium foil in a warm oven. The wax will melt off onto the foil. Leave the oven open to prevent overheating, smoke, or a possible wax fire

Scouring material should never be used on a fine metal mould. The inside of the mould must be unscratched so that candles will release easily. The experienced candlemaker will not even prod at the inside of a mould with a fingernail.

Mould holders, retaining screws, and rubber gaskets can be stored inside the moulds, but they should be wrapped in plastic so they don't scratch the mould.

Some candlemakers who are not purists don't clean their moulds at the end of the candlemaking operation. They announce – and with some justification – that enough mould release and wax remain on the moulds to prevent rusting. They simply wrap the moulds in plastic to keep the dust off and store them away.

Whether you store the moulds shining clean or daubed with wax, see that they are protected from dust.

Don't forget to remove the aluminium foil from the oven when you have finished cleaning your utensils. After the oven has cooled, examine it to make sure no drops of wax have got onto the oven floor or the walls.

Fold up the newspapers you have used in your work area and throw them away. Keeping wax-spattered paper is not a good idea because it is inflammable.

If you have got wax onto any item of clothing, remove the hardened wax with a table knife. Then either wash the clothing or send it to the cleaner's – explaining to the cleaner the sort of spot he has to deal with. The spot should come out.

Moulds

The novice candlemaker who starts out with one metal mould usually adds to his stock before long. The mould-makers offer a marvellous variety. There are tall moulds and short ones. Some are square and some are round and some are oval. There are hexagonal moulds and star-shaped moulds, moulds for squat candles and moulds for towering, tapered pillars of wax. And there are two- and three-part moulds in metal and in plastic (see page 34).

The professionally crafted mould is beautiful in itself. The candles cast in it are beautiful. But there is no reason why a candlemaker need confine himself to this sort of mould. Almost anything with a cavity in it can be a mould, and candlemaking is an endless experiment, anyway. So don't be inhibited. Experiment to your heart's content.

MOULDS AROUND THE HOME

How many moulds do you have? Look around your house. You may be surprised.

Do you have a fancy metal mould for jelly? Then you also have a metal mould for fancy candles.

A bun tray is handy for stack candles (see page 40).

Small fancy moulds are good if you want to make **'floaters'** – small candles which can be floated in water as part of a flower arrangement. The contours of the moulds are more interesting than those of plain baking containers like bun trays, and putting a wick into a floater is the easiest thing in the world. Use a small wire-core wick (see page 15) and insert it into the mould as the wax begins to harden in the mould. Hold the wick steady for a minute or two until the wax starts to scum. (Be sure the wick is in the centre of the mould, or your floater will burn unevenly and tilt to starboard.)

Pyrex baking dishes and custard moulds can be first-class moulds. They are heat-resistant and inexpensive, and they come in a number of sizes.

Ordinary glassware (not fine crystal, unless you don't mind risking it) can also be used to mould candles. For a pleasing, cone-shaped candle, try pouring wax into a lager glass. Juice glasses are good for small candles, and highball glasses will do for tall candles. The possibilities are endless. Open your cupboard doors and see what you have.

Bear one thing in mind when selecting moulds from your cupboard. You want to get your candle out of the glass – or the

Small fancy moulds are perfect for making candles which can be floated in water, either all by themselves or as part of a flower arrangement

Bun trays and fancy moulds take to hot wax readily. Glassware and plastic require more care. Pour into glass at about 76°C; if you use plastic, let your wax cool until a scum forms on top of it

fancy mould – once the wax has hardened. Containers which are wider at the top than at the bottom, such as lager glasses and fancy moulds, are easier when it comes to unmoulding. Containers with straight sides can be used, however. Coat the container with mould release before pouring wax. If the candle doesn't release after it has hardened, you need not give up and throw away the glass. Put it into hot water until the wax has softened, then turn the container upside down and let the wax slide out. Clean the glass as you would clean any candlemaking utensil – by putting it into a warm (not hot) oven, and then washing it.

Wicking after Unmoulding

Except for floaters, you will probably mould candles in bun trays, glasses, and pyrex dishes without wicks. Wicks can be inserted after a candle is unmoulded. Ue a wire-core wick. Dip it into warm wax and pull it taut. Then, with a heated skewer, make a wick hole in your candle. Insert the wire-core wick into this hole (see picture on page 15) and seal the hole by pouring a tiny bit of warm wax around the wick.

Well Areas

Cooling wax contracts and forms well areas in regular candle moulds. Cooling wax will also contract in a bun tray or a highball glass. The fact that you are moulding a candle without

If you want to use a glass container as a candle holder (see page 61), you should pre-wick the glass. Tie a wire-core wick to a wick holder and suspend the wick in the glass before filling it with wax. (You risk shattering the glass if you use a hot skewer to make a wick hole after wax has hardened)

wicking will not make the slightest difference – you will still have a depression in the centre of the wax. Reserve some melted wax, as you would if using a regular mould, and use it to fill this depression so that the top of the candle will be even.

Pouring Temperatures for Metal and Glass Moulds

Pouring temperatures for metal containers should be the same as for professional metal moulds – 82–93°C. If you use glass, let the wax cool at least to 77°C before pouring, and warm the glass first by putting it into the oven and setting the heat at low – very low. Leave the oven door open so that the glass doesn't overheat and shatter.

DISPOSABLE MOULDS

Though food packagers aren't often accused of thinking over-much about wax, many containers for food and drink make odd and interesting candle moulds.

Little tubs for soft margarine can become little tubs of wax – once the margarine has been eaten. Turn the hardened wax out of the margarine tub, add a wick (see page 15). and you have a chunky little candle.

Cardboard milk cartons have been with us for some time. If you have worked with a good square metal mould, a milk carton may seem clumsy, but don't overlook it entirely. Milk cartons do work fairly well, and if you want to mass-produce square candles, milk cartons can be handy indeed – and they can be disposed of without a qualm.

Don't throw away your empty beer or soft-drinks cans. They make very satisfactory moulds. Or check your stock of tinned vegetables and juices. Vegetable and juice tins come in all sizes, from tiny to jumbo.

An empty cottage-cheese container can be a candle mould, and so can an empty ice-cream carton.

Food containers aren't the only moulds the grocer provides. Even the cardboard core from a kitchen roll offers possibilities. Seal one end with a cardboard disc held in place with masking tape and you have a mould for a tall, slender candle. Coat the inside with release. (You won't be able to spray the inside of this mould, but you can pour in salad oil, swish it around, and then pour off the excess.) You will have to destroy the cardboard cylinder to get the candle out, but that's no problem. There will be another cardboard cylinder available as soon as you've used the next kitchen roll.

This candle is made of brown wax topped with white whipped wax which has been dribbled down the side for a realistic beer-stein effect. (See pages 59–60 for directions on whipping wax.) The glass was wicked before the wax was poured, as shown on page 31

Almost anything that will hold food can be a candle mould. Straight-sided containers and those with wide tops can be re-used. The unusual layered candle above was made in a cardboard carton which was cut away when the candle was unmoulded

Cottage-cheese cartons and beer or soft-drinks cans can be used again and again. If the container is wider at the top than at the bottom, or it has straight sides, the candle should release without difficulty. Always use mould release, and if there is an indentation at the top of a can which might bind the candle and prevent it from sliding out, remove this with a pair of metal cutters. However, don't try to use coffee tins to mould candles. Nearly all coffee tins have indentations running around the sides, and there's just no way to get a candle out.

Unmoulding Narrow-neck Moulds

If you greatly admire the shape of a plastic or glass container which has a narrow neck, you can use it as a mould if you don't mind destroying it when you release your candle. You might come across a well-designed pickle bottle or an elegant jar of mustard. After eating the pickles or using the mustard, clean the container well. If it's glass, warm it as you would any glass mould. Fill it with wax. The wax will contract and you will have to refill well cavities.

When the wax is completely hard, break the glass container. Wrap it in a piece of sheeting or in several layers of paper towels so that bits and pieces of glass can't fly around the kitchen. Then tap it gently with a hammer.

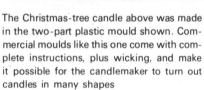

The Christmas-tree candle above was made in the two-part plastic mould shown. Commercial moulds like this one come with complete instructions, plus wicking, and make it possible for the candlemaker to turn out candles in many shapes

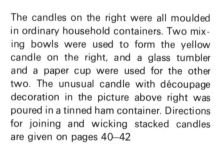

The candles on the right were all moulded in ordinary household containers. Two mixing bowls were used to form the yellow candle on the right, and a glass tumbler and a paper cup were used for the other two. The unusual candle with découpage decoration in the picture above right was poured in a tinned ham container. Directions for joining and wicking stacked candles are given on pages 40–42

Unmoulding Plastic Containers

Plastic won't break as glass does, and plastic bottles and jars can offer problems when used as candle moulds. The procedure for moulding is the same as that for moulding in glass bottles, but unmoulding is another matter. The plastic will have to be cut away from the candle with a sharp knife or a razor blade. Test the top edge of the container to see how easily it will cut. If you have encountered an especially tough piece of plastic, you may decide against attempting to mould a candle in that particular container.

Wicking Cardboard Moulds

When using food containers as moulds, it is often easier to pour the candle and let it harden, then unmould it and add a wire-core wick (see page 15). Cardboard containers can be wicked, however. With a skewer, make a small hole in the bottom of the container. Thread the wick through and tie a knot in it below the hole. Seal the wick hole with mould sealer or masking tape. Fasten the top of the wick to a wick holder. (This need not be a special object made only to hold wicks. A lollipop stick or a pencil will do. Tie the wick to the stick or pencil, or tape the wick to the holder with masking tape.)

Many hobby shops offer wick clips – little pieces of metal which are helpful in wicking a cardboard mould. They prevent the wick from breaking through into the mould.

Use a light touch when wicking cardboard. If you pull the wick too taut, you may pull out the bottom of the container, or crumple the top.

Pouring Temperatures for Cardboard and Plastic Moulds

When using cardboard moulds, let the melted wax cool almost to 63°C – or until it has a scum on the top – before you pour. If the wax is too hot, it may burst through the container.

Plastic containers can be slightly more heat-resistant than cardboard, but don't count on it. Cool the melted wax at least to 66°C before pouring into plastic. Pour a small bit at first, to see how well the plastic stands up. If it holds its shape, fine. Go ahead and fill the container. If it doesn't hold its shape, you have lost nothing but one disposable container, and you haven't spilled hot wax all over the kitchen counter.

Cardboard containers can be wicked before a candle is poured, and so can tin cans. Use a skewer to make a hole in the bottom. Thread the wick through the hole and fasten it to a wick holder laid across the top of the container. Seal the hole in the bottom with masking tape

Layered Candles

Leftover wax is no embarrassment. Candlemakers *always* have some wax left over, and there's no need to let this wax go to waste. Let it get hard, then break it into chunks and wrap the chunks in plastic so that they stay clean. You can remelt the wax and use it any time you want to.

Making a layered candle is one way to use leftover wax. Two different colours of wax are adequate for a layered candle. Three colours are more fun, and you can use as many as four or five. Suit yourself about colour combinations. A layered candle can be as muted or as mad as you please.

You must have more than one pouring container for a layered candle, since you must keep several batches of dyed wax molten at the same time. The pouring containers must have handles and pouring lips. Several of the smaller pyrex measuring cups or aluminium measuring jugs will take care of the situation without a huge outlay of money. (Don't try to pinch pennies and use old orange juice cans or vegetable tins. Without a lip on your pouring container, you can't pour layers of wax. You can try, but you won't like the results.)

Even if you have not amassed any great amount of leftover wax, you can make layered candles. Heat about 1 kg (2 lb) of medium-temperature paraffin wax in the top of a double boiler. Use a sugar thermometer. When the wax reaches 82°C, add stearin. When it reaches 93°C, remove the double boiler from the heat, wipe the bottom of the melting pot dry with paper towels, and divide the melted wax by pouring it into two, three, or more small pouring containers. Add dyes to the liquid wax in the pouring containers, and test for colour in the usual way (see page 18).

Keep the wax warm and molten by putting the pouring containers on trivets which have been placed in a pan of hot water. Almost everyone has a big, flat-bottomed roasting pan which can be used in this way. Bring the water in the pan to a boil, then turn the heat down so that the water just simmers. It isn't practical to clip a sugar thermometer to the rim of each and every pouring container, but if you use trivets and keep the water in the pan just under the boiling point, the wax in the containers will remain liquid and it won't overheat.

If you're using leftover wax, you can disregard the double boiler. Put chunks of dyed wax into the pouring containers and place these on the trivets in the pan of hot water. The wax will melt. And if you own an electric frying pan, you won't even need trivets.

Electric pans have automatic temperature controls. Put the pouring containers into the pan, fill the pan with water, set the temperature control at 93°C and don't worry. The warm water surrounding the pouring containers will keep the wax at an even temperature, and with that automatic control nothing can get too hot.

Horizontal Stripes

When pouring wax in layers, do not tilt the mould and pour down the side as you would if you were pouring a one-colour pillar candle. Pour carefully and directly into the bottom of the mould. Try not to splash wax on the wall of the mould.

Wicks and wick holders can get in the way of a good, clean pour, so pour into a wickless mould. If there is a hole in the bottom of the mould, seal it with masking tape or mould sealer.

After pouring the first layer of coloured wax, let it set and harden a bit. For a clear-cut line of separation between colours, the first layer of wax should be quite firm before the second layer is poured. For a gentler blending of colour, the second layer can be poured while the first layer is still warm. Test the hardness of the first layer of wax by prodding it in the centre with a pencil or the handle of a wooden spoon. The wax should be slightly tacky even if you want a sharp separation between your coloured layers. It can be almost liquid if you want the colours to blend into one another.

A candle poured in layers will contract and sag in the middle just as surely as any other candle. Don't let this worry you. Save some wax when you pour the last layer. After the candle has set and the depression appears in the centre of this last layer, use your reserved wax to fill the depression and even off the top of the candle.

Water baths are not usually used for layered candles. Let the candle remain in the mould overnight, to make sure it is completely cold, then unmould it.

Wicking

Add a wick, using a hot skewer to make a wick hole. A wire-core wick will insert most easily. The size depends on the size of the layered candle.

Diagonal Stripes

The easiest layered candle to make is one with regular horizontal stripes. A variation on this is the diagonally striped candle. You get diagonal stripes by tilting your mould.

Rest one side of the mould on a support. The support need not be any complicated gadget. It need only be stable. A medium-

A variation on the layered candle is the one with diagonal stripes of colour. The process is exactly the same as for layering, except that the mould is tilted as shown. The support for the mould can be very simple, but it must be stable

thick paperback book or a little stack of magazines will do.

Pour a layer of colour into the mould and let the wax set. Then pour a second layer of colour and let that set. If you're working with a third or fourth colour, pour those layers. When the first three or four layers are firm, turn your mould and tilt it in the opposite direction, using the paperback book or the stack of magazines to keep it steady.

Pour several layers of colour, letting each set between pourings.

Tilt the mould again, if you wish.

When the layered wax has nearly reached the top of the mould, set the mould level. The last pouring should be all one colour, and it must be poured when the mould is on the level. Reserve a little wax to fill any depression which may appear in the top of the candle.

The diagonally striped candle is unmoulded and wicked just as the regular candle is unmoulded and wicked. Make sure it has completely hardened before you remove it from the mould.

Mottling

If you want a mottled look in your layered candles, you can get it by adding oil to your melted wax just before pouring. No special mottling oil is needed. Almost any oil will mottle wax. Use a good quality oil, however – such as the fine machine oil used on sewing machines. Three teaspoons of oil to $\frac{1}{2}$ kg (1 lb) of wax will be adequate.

Pouring

It is not wise to pour half of a layered candle one day and the second half another day. Once the layers of wax you poured on Day One cool and harden completely, they may not be receptive to the layers of wax you pour on Day Two. Cold wax is brittle, and it tries not to adhere to warm wax. If you start to pour wax in layers, finish in one grand operation – or you may have a candle which will do its best to break in half. You may also ruin the layered surface. Cold wax can pull away from the walls of the mould, and warm wax added to layers of cold wax can seep down between the cold wax and the mould and spoil the design of the candle. It can also bind the candle into the mould.

Stacked Candles

Cold wax tries not to adhere to warm wax. That is a fact of life and something a candlemaker needs to remember. Once the candlemaker knows the rules, he can often find ways to break them – or at least to work around them. The proof of this is the stack candle, which is moulded in several parts and then put together with hot wax and wicking.

The most basic stack candle is the bun-tray candle. All of the depressions in a bun tray are the same size and the same shape. All are wider at the top than at the bottom. Wax rounds moulded in a bun tray will not vary more than a hair one from another.

Begin construction of a stacked candle as you would begin any candle. Heat wax. Add stearin and dye. Remove wax from the heat.

Coat your mould – in this case the bun-tray – with mould release.

Now pour. Fill each little cup in the bun-tray with hot wax.

Forget the water bath. Bun trays are shallow and you might get water into the wax if you tried to put a bun tray into a bath.

Let the wax in the bun cups set. The wax will shrink as it cools. Fill any depressions that appear so that all the bun cups are level and full to the brim.

Wait until the wax buns are solid and the bun tray is cool to the touch. Then unmould the wax by turning the bun tray upside down. The wax rounds should slide out easily, since bun trays were made for easy unmoulding.

Wicking

Calculate the exact centre of your round wax buns. This doesn't require an advanced degree in mathematics. Use a ruler and measure the width of the rounds. Halfway across is the centre, and you can mark this by jabbing a pencil point into the wax.

With a hot skewer, make a wick hole through the centre of each round of wax.

A metal wick clip is a great help in wicking a stack candle. Select the wax round which will be the base of the candle. Use an electric pen or a soldering iron, if you have one, to make an indentation in the bottom of this round for the wick clip. If you don't have one of these, almost any implement which can be heated will do the job. You need only to melt away a bit of the wax. Try a screwdriver or a tin opener. (Don't use a paring knife; heating a knife blade can destroy the cutting edge.)

Insert the wick clip into the bottom of the wax round.

Cut a piece of wicking which will be several centimetres longer than the finished stacked candle. Knot one end of this wick. Thread the wick through the wick clip and the wick hole in the base of the candle. Pull the wick taut, so that the knot is right up against the wick clip.

Heat paraffin wax to 93°C. Since cold wax does not want to stick to warm wax, make sure the wax which will fasten your stacked candle together is not just warm. It should be *hot*. Also, you may fare better if the pouring container for this hot wax has a spout rather than simply a pouring lip. The measuring cup will answer the purpose, but a small kettle with a spout will be neater, easier, and safer. Heat the wax right in the pouring container – over boiling water, of course – and use the sugar thermometer.

Pour a little of the hot wax into the wick hole in the base of your candle.

Thread a second wax bun onto the top of the wick. Do not immediately push this second round of wax down onto the round which will be the base of the candle. Wait for just a moment – long enough to pour a goodly dollop of that clear, hot paraffin wax on top of the base of the candle. (Watch your fingers; that's *hot* wax.) Then quickly slide the second wax round down the wick and press it against the first round in the stack. The hot wax will seal the two wax buns together.

Pour a little hot wax into the wick hole of the second wax round.

Thread a third wax bun onto the wick.

Pour hot wax on top of the second wax bun and quickly slide the third round of wax into position on top of the second round.

Repeat this process, stacking one wax bun on top of another and sealing them into place with hot wax, until you have run through your supply of wax buns or until your candle is as tall as you want it to be.

If any wax has dribbled or spurted out from between the sections of your stacked candle, it will have hardened by now and can be easily removed with a paring knife – or perhaps even with a finger nail.

Glazing

Holding the candle by the long wick, dip it into hot wax for a good glaze (see page 25), and also for added insurance that the stack will remain in one piece. Remember to allow for displacement when you dip the stack. The level of wax in your glazing container will rise as the candle is dipped.

Let the glaze harden, then trim off the extra wick.

Stacking

Stacked candles which are moulded in bun trays can be put together so that the wide part of each wax round is matched to the wide part of the next wax round, and the narrow parts of the rounds are matched to the narrow parts. But there isn't any requirement that the stack be assembled this way. You can turn all the rounds one way. You can wick the stack so that it is a series of upside-down wax buns. You can use all one colour, or different colours. You can use a clear glaze or you can add dye to your glaze. You can do it any way you please.

In fact, you do not even need a bun tray. All the elements in your stack of wax need not be the same size. Baking dishes come in graduated sizes and make beautiful moulds for stacked candles.

At a certain point, common sense will set in. If you use moulds of different sizes for a stacked candle, plan to use the largest wax round (or square, or whatever) as the base of the stack. The candle will be much more stable.

Also, do not try to combine shapes which have no relation to one another. Piling squares on top of rounds on top of ball shapes will not be very pleasing, and no matter how expertly you wick and seal the parts, you're apt to have a lopsided candle. Lopsided candles don't burn nicely. They fall over, and they sometimes break apart.

In assembling your stacked candle, use plenty of wick to allow for easier handling when you glaze. Make sure the wick hole is in the centre of each wax round

Chunk Candles

To make a chunk candle, you need all your regular candlemaking supplies and you also need chunks of wax. The chunks should be coloured, because colourless chunks are no fun at all. Beyond that, the approach to chunks depends on the temperament of the candlemaker.

If you have leftover wax, you may already have chunks. If you don't have leftover wax, you can make chunks.

Making Chunks

Heat medium-temperature paraffin wax in a melting pot or double boiler. Use a sugar thermometer. When the wax reaches 82°C, stir in stearin. Add dye and test for colour.

Coat a flat-bottomed container with mould release. Candlemakers sometimes suggest using a baking sheet for chunks, but baking sheets are large. Unless you want heaps of chunks, a square sandwich tin is satisfactory.

Pour the hot, dyed wax into the sandwich tin. How much you pour is up to you. How thick do you want your chunks to be? You can pour one centimetre of wax, or two centimetres, or more than three.

If you want free-form chunks, your task is simple. Let the wax in the tin get completely cold, then turn it out and break it up with a hammer.

If you want chunks that are more restrained – small squares or strips of wax – you will have to cut them. Don't let the wax in the tin get cold and hard. Let it solidify, but start cutting chunks while the wax is still warm and malleable. Using a paring knife to cut the warm wax, and work from the outer edge of the tin towards the centre, since the wax in the centre will not harden as quickly as the wax round the edges.

If you find that you have miscalculated, and the wax in the pan is too brittle to cut, you can start again. Remelt the wax, pour it into the tin, and again wait for it to set.

After you have cut all the wax in the tin into chunks, let the chunks get thoroughly hard, then turn the tin upside down. The chunks will drop out.

Once you have chunks, you can proceed to make a chunk candle.

With one or two exceptions, chunk candles are made exactly the way all moulded candles are made. Prepare your work area and wick your mould in the usual manner.

Melt medium-temperature paraffin wax in a melting pot or double boiler, using a sugar thermometer.

Chunks for your chunk candle can be as thick or as thin as you please. Cut them from a square sandwich tin as the molten wax begins to harden, working from the outer edge of pan towards centre. (The wax in the centre remains liquid longest)

Do not add stearin. Stearin makes wax opaque. You have gone to some trouble to achieve chunks, and you want them to show through the walls of your finished candle. So omit stearin.

If you use dye – and you probably will, since undyed wax looks grey – use it sparingly and choose a colour that will complement your chunks – light yellow for orange chunks, or pale pink for hot pink chunks.

Pouring

When the wax in the melting pot is ready – that is, when dye has been added and the wax is at about 82°C – put a handful of chunks into the mould. Pour liquid wax over these. Chunk candles are usually poured a little at a time, and two or three centimetres are as much as you should attempt on the first pour.

Omit the water bath. Let the wax set around the chunks in the mould. Prod between the chunks with your skewer and fill any air cavities that appear.

When the first pouring has set, add more chunks and more wax. Let the second pouring harden and fill air cavities.

Then add more chunks and more wax. Repeat until you have filled your mould or run out of chunks or liquid wax.

Let the candle remain in the mould overnight, then unmould and finish it as you would any other candle – trimming excess wax off the bottom with a cheese grater and rubbing the bottom on a hot griddle to smooth it. Cut off extra wick.

Variations

The chunk candle can be varied in several ways. For example, chunks made without stearin will melt more quickly than chunks containing stearin, and the candlemaker can use them for a marbled effect. He can put them in a mould and pour on very hot wax, so that the chunks blend and run together, colouring the candle from within. The smaller the chunks, the more easily they will melt and blend.

If you want to avoid marbling, add extra stearin to the wax you will use for chunks. When the chunks have set and are in the mould, don't cover them with very hot wax. Let the liquid wax cool to 75°C or less.

If you are not satisfied with the showing your chunks make inside the finished candle, you can remove some of the wax from the surface of the candle by dipping the candle into hot water. Remember to allow for displacement. Use hot, but not boiling, water and be sure you have plenty of extra wick protruding from the candle. The best and safest way to dip a candle is to hold it by the wick.

Put wax chunks into wicked mould a handful at a time. A couple of centimetres of chunks in the mould is enough to start. Then pour melted, dyed wax over chunks. When set, repeat

Lace Candles

Wax and water will not mix, and because of this we have lace candles. The lace candle, which is also called the ice candle, consists of an inner candle or core candle surrounded by a shell of wax which has irregular holes in it. When the lace candle is lighted, the core candle will burn down into the wax shell, and the light will gleam out through the holes.

To make a lace candle, you should have a large-diameter mould. Your core candle can be an ordinary taper, bought at a store. It should not be taller than your mould, and when it is inserted into the centre of the mould, there should be more than 2·5 cms (1 in) of space between the core candle and the walls of the mould.

Wicking is no problem with a lace candle, since the core candle comes already wicked. You will get good results if you use a good metal mould, but seal the hole in the bottom of the mould with masking tape.

Melt medium-temperature paraffin wax in a double boiler or melting pot. Use a sugar thermometer and add stearin and dye when the wax reaches 82°C.

Pour about 1·25 cms (½ in) of liquid wax into the bottom of the mould. Set the bottom of the core candle in this wax and hold it steady, making sure it is in the centre of the mould. The wax will harden around it and secure it.

Turn out a tray of ice cubes. Wrap the ice cubes in a towel and tap them with a hammer. Don't pulverize the ice. If each cube breaks into two or three pieces, your ice will do its part in making beautiful waxen lace.

For a lace candle, put cracked ice into a mould around the core candle. Start with about 3 cms (2 ins) of ice. Pour wax over ice until the ice is almost covered. When set, repeat

Pouring

Drop this cracked ice into the mould until it surrounds the core candle to a depth of about 7·5 cms (3 ins).

Pour melted wax over the cracked ice until the wax almost covers the ice.

Wait until this poured wax has hardened slightly, then add more cracked ice and more melted wax. Repeat, until the layers of ice and wax are level with the top of the core candle.

After the last pouring, you can hasten the cooling of the lace candle by putting the mould into a water bath for an hour or so. You do not need to test for well areas, since the core candle will not have any, and the outer wax shell is already full of holes.

Remove the mould from the water bath and let the candle cool at room temperature for six to eight hours.

Unmoulding

It is a good idea to unmould a lace candle in the sink. Fold a dish towel to several thicknesses and put it in the sink. Tap the mould gently against this towel. The candle should slide out. All the ice will have turned to water, and this will run out of the candle.

Make sure that no pockets of water remain in the candle. Examine the lace shell carefully. If it appears that water has been trapped inside the wax, heat your trusty skewer, make a small hole in the wax, and drain off the water.

Dry your mould carefully, and treat it with mould release to prevent rust.

There are purists who say that the core candle and the lace shell should be the same colour. They certainly can be, but you can also experiment with contrasts. Try a red core candle and a white wax shell, or an orange candle with green lace, or any combination that appeals to you.

Burning

When a lace candle is lighted, there is always a possibility that molten wax from the burning core candle will run out through the holes in the lace shell. This can be very attractive, but use a large enough candle holder to allow for this. It is possible to remove wax stains from a tablecloth, but it's much easier simply to remove spilled wax from a candle holder.

Hurricane Candles

Hurricane candles aren't candles at all, since they have no wicks and they are not intended to be burned. A hurricane candle is a wax shell, and the best hurricane candles are cast in metal moulds made especially for this purpose. They are large moulds and they have no wick holes.

If you already have a good, big metal mould, you can make a hurricane candle in it. Close the wick hole in the bottom of the mould with masking tape.

It takes a large amount of wax to cast a hurricane candle. Allow at least 2·3 litres (2 quarts), or 2·4 kgs (5½ lb). Prepare the wax as usual, melting it over boiling water and using a sugar thermometer. When the wax reaches 93°C, add dye. *Do not add stearin.* When the hurricane candle is finished, a votive light will be placed inside it. The glow from the votive light should shine through the wax hurricane shell, and so you want it to be translucent. Stearin would make it opaque.

Spray the hurricane mould with mould release and pour the melted wax into the mould to the desired height. Be sure to stop pouring when the wax is about 2·5 cms (1 in) from the top of the mould.

Put the mould in a water bath and weigh it down if necessary.

Once the mould is in the water bath, watch it carefully. When the wax hardens across the top, start testing it with a knife. The walls of a hurricane candle will be about 1 cm (½ in) thick when the wax on the top of the candle is 6 mm (¼ in) thick. That's the time to go into action.

With your paring knife, cut the hardened wax from the top of the candle. Insert the knife into the wax 1 cm (½ in) in from the wall of the mould and cut all the way around the mould, keeping the knife 1 cm away from the wall. Then lift the layer of solid wax off the top of the candle.

Remove the mould from the water bath and dry the outside.

Pour the liquid wax from the mould into the melting pot.

What remains in the hurricane mould is a shell of wax about 1 cm (½ in) thick. This is your hurricane candle.

Allow it to cool for four or five hours inside the mould, then unmould it.

There may be some ragged spots on the top edge of the candle. These can be trimmed away with a knife, or they can be melted away by rubbing the edges of the candle gently on a hot griddle.

Put a votive candle inside the hurricane shell and light the votive candle. Then sit back and enjoy the glow.

A large-diameter candle and a small votive candle can be combined to simulate a hurricane candle. Let the wick in the large candle burn down an inch or two. Scoop out the molten wax. Repeat to depth desired. Put votive light into the resulting cavity. Its glow will shine through the walls of the larger candle

Free-form candles are fun. Plastic sheeting was used to mould the candle on the right, and aluminium foil moulded the candle below (see page 52 for directions). You can also make free-form candles in sand moulds (see page 53)

Free-form Candles

Almost anything with a cavity in it can be a candle mould, and for casting candles in odd and unusual shapes, some rather unusual material can be used.

There is plastic, for example. Plastic bowls and food containers are familiar to us, but there are also sheets of plastic. It covers the clothes that come from the cleaner. Most of us have rolls of it in our kitchen. We use it to wrap food.

At first glance, plastic sheeting would seem to be about the most unlikely material on earth to use for a candle mould. It looks as if it would melt at about 12°C. It won't. It's tougher than that, and if a candlemaker exercises care, he can use it to fashion candles in some interesting shapes.

First, spray the plastic with mould release.

Next, make a cavity into which you can pour wax. This is simple. Push the plastic down into a glass jar. Let the edges hang out around the top of the jar. Slip a rubber band onto the top of the jar to hold the plastic in place.

Melt your wax in a double boiler or melting pot, adding stearin and dye when the wax reaches 82°C. Remove wax from the heat. Let it cool until a scum forms on the surface.

Pouring

Carefully pour a little wax into the plastic cavity you have created inside the glass jar. If the wax melts through the plastic, you'll have to find another kind of plastic sheet. The chances are, however, that the wax won't melt through, and you can go ahead and fill the plastic sack with warm wax.

Allow the wax to cool for a short time. When it's no longer liquid, but still soft and pliable, remove the sack from the jar.

Close the top of the plastic container by bringing the ends together, giving them a slight twist and securing them with a piece of string or with the rubber band. Now you have a plastic bag filled with pliable wax. You can twist it, knead it, prod it, poke it, and mould it into any shape you want.

When you're satisfied with the shape of the wax, put the plastic sack into cool water and allow the wax to get hard.

Unmould your free-form candle by removing the string or rubber band and peeling the plastic away from the wax.

Wicking

Use a hot skewer to make a wick hole in the mass of wax. Insert a wire-core wick (see page 15). If necessary, smooth the bottom by rubbing on a hot griddle.

When making a free-form candle in plastic sheeting, allow the wax to cool until it can be handled easily and safely, then remove it from its supporting jar to mould it into whatever shape you want

Casting in Foil

Aluminium foil is not nearly as malleable as plastic, but it is an excellent material for receiving hot wax. It is almost impossible to damage foil, and the candlemaker can pour into a foil container without fear of a wax break-through.

You can use foil as you would use plastic. Suspend a foil sack in a jar and fill it with hot wax. When the wax has cooled, but before it gets hard, remove the foil sack and shape the wax by hand. When the wax is solid, peel away the foil and wick the resulting free-form candle.

Be prepared for crinkles in the surface of the candle. Foil *will* crinkle. If you don't like the effect, remove it by dipping the candle into hot wax. (Make sure the wick is thoroughly set in the candle before you dip.)

Quieter adventures are possible when you mould with foil. You can fill a dish-pan or an old pot with sand. Scoop out enough sand to make a depression to receive the foil mould. Push the foil into that depression and fill the resulting foil mould with hot wax. The sand will support the mould until the wax sets.

Foil-cast candles poured in layers are very popular. Interesting shapes can be achieved by creasing the foil before pouring the wax. After the candle is unmoulded, the surface will be clean and glossy.

Wicking

It is easy to add a wick to a foil-cast candle after the candle is unmoulded. But if you wish, you can wick a foil mould before you pour wax. Put a stick across the top of the mould and fasten a wire-core wick to this. Pull the wick straight and pour wax around it. As it cools, the wax will sag around the wick. Test for well areas and add hot wax to fill in the sagging depression.

Foil can be used for free-form candles in exactly the same manner as plastic. For wicking, use a hot skewer and a wire-core wick. (See page 15)

Sand-cast Candles

There are almost no limits to what an imaginative candlemaker can do with sand and wax. Sand-cast candles can be deep or shallow, layered, mottled, decorated, plain, glazed or unglazed, carefully shaped or delightfully free.

For sand-casting, you will need all the candle equipment you have (except moulds), and you will also need sand. Nice, clean sand is what is required – sand free of small sticks and bits of leaves and other unsightly stuff. Go to the nearest builders' supply company and look over the stock. Select what appeals to you and bring the sand home.

Prepare the wax in the usual way – melting, adding stearin and dye, watching your sugar thermometer.

Preparing the Mould

While the wax is melting, prepare your sand mould. Put your sand into a container and add water. The sand must be damp, or it will not hold any shape at all. It shouldn't be so wet that it's runny, but it must be thoroughly damp all the way through.

Make a cavity in the damp sand. If you want a free-form candle, you will use your hands to make the cavity. If you're feeling more formal, press some object into the sand so that the cavity will have a definite shape. A bowl or a vase can be used to shape sand. (Naturally, you will remove the object from the sand before you pour wax.)

When the hole in the sand is pleasing to you, and the wax is ready, fill the hole with liquid wax.

As the candle sets, fill any sags and wells that appear.

Let the candle remain in the sand mould overnight.

Unmould the candle by removing the wax from the sand. Since sand can be messy, do the unmoulding outside.

Make a wick hole with a hot skewer and insert a wire-core wick – and there's your sand candle!

Variations

There are endless, delightful variations on this basic process, and you will probably think of more as you work with sand and wax.

You may want a candle with a thick crust of sand. If you do, pour wax into the sand mould at 93°C.

If you don't want a very thick crust on your sand-cast candle, pour cooler wax – at about 66°C.

If you want a free-form candle with almost no sand on it, take the candle out of doors and turn a hose on it. Some of the sand will wash away. What remains can be removed. Either dip the candle into hot water (making sure that the wick is firmly embedded in the wax, and allowing for displacement) or get a propane torch. Small propane torches are not expensive, and they are marvellous for glazing large candles, for removing unwanted patches of sand, and for softening and sculpturing free-form candles.

One wick is adequate for a sand-cast candle, but more than one can be inserted into the candle if the candle is large.

You can fashion a candle for which sand is a container. Mix melted wax with dry sand. Add enough wax to make the mixture like dough, and work quickly before the wax can harden.

Spray mould release into a bowl or a foil mould.

Line the bowl or the mould with the combination of wax and sand, pressing the mixture against the mould with your fingers.

Allow the wax and sand mixture in the mould to harden.

Pour coloured, perfumed wax into this sand mould.

After the resulting candle has hardened, remove it from the bowl or the mould. Use your skewer (heated) to make a wick hole and insert a wire-core wick.

Sand for the sand-cast candle must be thoroughly damp all the way through. If you are making a free-form candle, you can use your hands to make a cavity in the sand (left). After the wax has hardened, un-mould your sand-cast candle by removing it from the sand

Flower Candles

Candles with flowers embedded in them are somewhat like lace candles in that they are made in two parts. There is a centre candle – a core candle – and an outer shell of wax which contains the floral decorations.

To make a flower candle, you need all the usual candlemaking supplies, a core candle, a fairly large-diameter mould, and some flowers and leaves.

If you wish, make the core candle yourself. The size is up to you, but the core candle must be about 2·5 cms (1 in) less in diameter than the mould for the flower candle. It is perfectly legitimate to buy a pillar candle and use it for the core candle, but keep in mind the relative size of the mould and the core candle. You will need that inch of room.

Pin flowers and leaves to the core candle.

Wicking

Insert the core candle into the mould, wick first. Thread the wick through the wick hole in the bottom of the mould and secure it by sealing the hole with masking tape.

If you are using a pillar candle which you have purchased for the core candle, threading that bit of wick through a wick hole may be a challenge. Help yourself along by tying a string to the wick, threading that through the hole and drawing the core candle after it.

If you are using a candle which you yourself have made for a core candle, leave lots of extra wick on top of the candle and thread this through the wick hole in the bottom of the mould. Then insert the core candle with the flowers pinned to it, draw the wick tight at the bottom of the mould and secure it with masking tape.

Melt paraffin wax and add dye that will blend with the colour of your inner core candle. Don't add stearin; you want the outer wax shell of the candle to be translucent so that the flowers will show through.

Pouring

Pour wax into the space between the core candle and the wall of the mould. Pouring temperature should be about 82°C. You can use a water bath if you wish, but it isn't really necessary. Watch the wax set, prod around the core candle with your skewer and fill any well areas that appear.

When the flower candle is cold – after several hours – unmould it as you would any candle.

For a flower candle, you need a core candle, a large-diameter mould, plastic flowers and leaves, and pins for fastening flowers to the candle

After pinning flowers and leaves to the core candle, put the candle into your mould and pour warm wax into the space between mould and candle

Be sparing with dyes when making a flower candle. Pale colours like pink, yellow, light blue, and white are best, since they will not compete too strongly with the colour of the flowers.

Plastic flowers are also best, since real flowers may wilt when exposed to hot wax. You need not confine yourself to plastic flowers, however. Experiment. Try dried leaves, bits of pine branch, or any piece of greenery that appeals to you.

If you want your flower candle to have an 'exfoliated' look – that is, if you want the surface of the flowers to extend beyond the surface of the candle – melt away some of the wax shell surrounding the core candle by rolling in hot water – hot, not boiling.

For an exfoliated candle, it is possible to avoid the two-step process. Pin flowers to the surface of a pillar candle, then dip the candle into a glaze of warm wax. Remember to allow for displacement, and don't worry about the pins. They won't show through the wax, and part of the fun of candlemaking is finding ways to cheat.

For best results, make sure that the plastic flowers in your flower candle touch the walls of the mould so they will show through the outer wax shell. Use a pastel colour for the wax shell, and don't use any stearin

Ball Candles

In November, when the Christmas decorations go up in the department stores, the urge to make round candles often sweeps over candlemakers. A wax snowball with a wick in it is a charming Christmas gift, and it doesn't cost the earth.

To make a ball candle, you need a round mould. Ordinary household containers like mixing bowls have a way of not being truly round. Check your cupboards; if you find a bowl or cup with a round bottom, you are in business. If you don't – and you probably won't – you can still be in business. There are a number of approaches to ball candles. Choose the one that suits you.

Two-part Moulds

You can visit the hobby shop and buy a round mould. These are two-part moulds. There are metal moulds and plastic moulds for ball candles, and the moulds come complete with instructions as to assembling, wicking and pouring temperatures. (If the mould is metal, the pouring temperature will be the same as for any metal mould – that is, about 82–93°C.)

Prepare the wax as you would for any candle. Pour the melted wax into the wicked mould. Let it begin to set, then break the surface tension with your skewer and fill any well areas, just as you would if you were pouring a pillar candle. When the candle has cooled completely, unmould it by opening the two-part mould. Remove any seam line with a paring knife and, if necessary, flatten the bottom of the ball candle by rubbing it on a hot griddle.

Making Your Own Plaster-of-Paris Mould

If you decide not to invest in a two-part ball mould, you can still pour round candles. Make your own half-round moulds using plaster of Paris. Get a ball that is the size you want your candle to be. A visit to a toy shop or a department store will take care of that. The best ball for this purpose is one with a seam running round the centre. It saves all sorts of trouble; you don't have to work out exactly how much ball is half a round.

The plaster of Paris comes from the hobby shop with instructions for mixing and pouring.

Prepare the plaster of Paris and pour it into a container. Let it set slightly and then put the ball into it. Press down until the plaster covers exactly half the ball. Let the plaster of Paris harden, then remove the ball.

Now get another container, prepare another batch of plaster

Two half-round moulds can be used for a ball candle. Shape the moulds by pressing a ball into containers of plaster of Paris. After moulding two half-rounds of wax, cut a groove across one, lay the wick into the groove, then fasten the halves together with very hot wax – about 93°C

of Paris, let it set slightly and then press the ball into it until half the ball is covered. After the plaster has hardened, remove the ball.

You now have two half-round moulds. After they have dried completely, coat the cavities with mould release and fill them with hot wax. As the wax cools and settles, be sure to fill the centres with melted wax so that the finished halves of the ball will fit together perfectly.

Wicking

When the wax is hard, turn it out of the moulds. With a knife, make a groove along the centre of the flat surface of one half-ball. Lay a wick in this groove and pour very hot wax – 93°C – over the flat surface and the wick. Then quickly press the second half-ball of wax onto the first to form a complete ball of wax.

Let the candle harden completely so that the two halves are firmly joined and the wick is solidly set in the candle. Smooth away any seam line with a paring knife and trim off extra wick. Flatten the bottom of the candle by rubbing it on a hot griddle.

Disposable Glass Moulds

In addition to two-part metal or plastic moulds and do-it-yourself plaster-of-Paris moulds, there are glass breakaway moulds available for ball candles. These are round glass vials with narrow necks for receiving melted wax. They must be destroyed as the candle is unmoulded, but they are not expensive and they are easy to use for smaller ball candles. Simply set them in a container of sand to hold them upright, pour in wax at about 82°C, watch the wax set, and break the surface tension so that you can fill any well areas that appear. When the wax is cold, unmould the ball candle by breaking the glass (gently, so that you don't crack the candle). Trim away any excess wax that may have collected around the area of the pouring spout with a knife. Make a wick hole with a hot skewer and add a wire-core wick to the candle.

One of the nicest snowball candles is a red candle frosted with white whipped wax. If you want an all-white candle, or a blue one, or even a lavender one, that's up to you, but the red snowball with white frosting is the odds-on favourite.

Whipped Wax

Make wax frosting by whipping warm wax just as you'd whip cream. Melt the wax in the top of the double boiler and add a goodly amount of stearin so it will be nice and white. Let the wax cool until scum forms on the top. With an electric mixer or a rotary egg beater, whip this scum until it becomes a lather.

After the two halves of this ball candle were put together, it was dipped in bright red wax

This ball candle was made by filling a Christmas ornament with wax, then breaking the ornament after the wax hardened

Then spoon it out and frost the snowball with it exactly as you would frost a cake.

Don't try to whip an entire pot of wax at one time. Beat the top layer of scum and use that. Work quickly, so that the whipped wax doesn't harden before you can get it onto the candle. While you are frosting the snowball, a second layer of scum will be forming on the melted wax. Whip that after you have used up the lather from the first layer. You can whip a third batch and a fourth batch and a fifth if you need to, and if the wax in the double boiler gets too solid for whipping, you can put it back on the heat and melt it again.

Clean the egg beater or the blades of the electric mixer by putting them on foil in a warm oven to melt off the wax. Then wash them in hot water and soap.

One classic way to use whipped wax is to frost a ball candle and make a Christmas snowball. Another is to fill a sundae glass for a parfait candle. Parfait candles can be all whipped wax (strawberry is a nice colour) or part plain wax, as here. A white whipped-wax topping looks like whipped cream. The beer-stein candle on page 32 is a variation on this, except that the power of suggestion turns the wax to white foam

Candles in Containers

Not all candles are meant to be unmoulded. Parfait candles like the one on the facing page and beer-stein candles (see page 32) remain in their sundae glasses and steins, and any nice container – from a pickle jar to a flowerpot to a covered sweet dish – can be a candle holder if *you* decide that it is. Fill it with wax and wick, and light it.

There are only a few special things to remember when making candles that are to be burned in the containers in which they are moulded:

Use a lower-temperature wax so that the candle will burn evenly all the way across and will use itself up entirely as it burns.

If you value the container, don't try to insert the wick after you have poured the wax. Pre-wick the candle using the method illustrated on page 31.

If you are using a clear glass container, use a dyed wax. For a coloured glass container, a clear or very lightly coloured wax will work best. If your container is opaque, like the flowerpot shown here, use the colours that suit you – and the container.

After burning the candle, you can clean the container as you would any candlemaking utensil. Put it into a warm oven and let the leftover wax melt off onto a sheet of foil.

Glassware, cheese crocks, flowerpots, openwork bricks or cement blocks (see the example on page 2) – any of these can be used as attractive and unusual candle holders

Decorating Candles

There is almost no end to the things that can be done with wax to make candles more personal, more decorative, and more special. For example:

Pour a very thin layer of red wax onto a pie plate. With a tiny biscuit cutter, cut out tiny hearts as the wax begins to harden. Press the hearts to a white pillar candle while they are still soft, and fuse the edges against the candle with a hot skewer. (The same general procedure – using different shapes and different colours – was used to decorate the appliqué candle at the top left of the facing page.)

Dip a white taper into intensely dyed liquid wax. Let the layer of dyed wax harden for a few minutes and then dip the taper again. Punch polka dots out of the still-soft layer of dyed wax with the blunt end of a pencil.

Apply photographs, prints, lettering, or any paper pattern to a candle. Heat clear wax, then dip the paper into the wax with tweezers. Apply it quickly to the candle. When it is set in place, dip the entire candle for a smooth finish.

Pin flowers and leaves or paper lace to the outside of a candle. Sequins, fake jewels, seed pearls, and cotton lace also make good pin-on decorations.

Paint your own design on a plain candle. The hobby shops offer paints manufactured especially for use on candles. These can be applied with a camel's-hair brush, and they dry instantly. Painted candles can be finished by dipping them into a clear glaze.

Dribble brightly coloured wax over a pastel candle. There are waxes especially made for this purpose. Called 'dribble waxes', they are softer and more adhesive than regular paraffin wax, and some fluorescent colours are available. You can dribble wax over the top of the candle, letting it run down the sides, or you can place the candle on its side and dribble so that the coloured wax encircles the candle (see the examples on page 5).

Whip a batch of wax (see pages 59–60) and use it to fasten a three-dimensional ornament to a candle. Lay the candle on its side, apply a blob of whipped wax, then embed the ornament in the wax. Let the entire thing harden before standing the candle erect, or the whipped wax may run down the side of the candle.

These ideas are only beginnings. From here on, you're on your own. Use your imagination. Let yourself go. Have fun!

These are just a few of the many creative possibilities for decorating the outside of candles. Directions (and more ideas) will be found on the facing page. But be sure to experiment on your own — it's half the fun!

Also available in this series

FRAMING
MACRAMÉ
RUGMAKING
POTTERY
WEAVING
JEWELLERY
CROCHET

Suppliers of candlemaking materials

GREAT BRITAIN
Candlemaking materials are stocked by very few handi-
craft shops in Great Britain, but all materials are
available by post from:

Atlas Handicrafts Ltd
PO Box 27
Laurel Street
Preston PR1 3XS

Candle Kit
129 Rosendale Road
West Dulwich
London SE21 8HE
who will send a price list on receipt of a stamped and
addressed envelope

Candlemaker's Supplies
4 Beaconsfield Terrace Road
(off Blythe Road)
London W14 0PP

Dryad Ltd
Northgate
Leicester LE1 4QR

Legendcraft
21 Coombe Road
Otford, Kent

Wincan
369 Church Lane
Kingsbury
London NW9

Materials in large quantities are also available from
the following sources:

Oil soluble dyes
Sandoz Products Limited
208 Acton Lane
London NW10

Stearin
Wynmouth Lehr and Fatoils Limited
158 City Road
London EC1

Waxes
Burmah Oil Waxes Limited
Thames Road, Crayford, Kent

Poth, Hille and Company Limited
High Street
Stratford, London E15

Wicks
Hayes and Finch Limited
30/38 Vernon Street
Liverpool